a guided poetry journal

SOUTH OF WONDERLAND

A JOURNEY OF SELF-DISCOVERY THROUGH JOURNALING & GOAL SETTING

NORTH OF DESPAIR

Windi Floyd Reynolds

SOUTH OF WONDERLAND

NORTH OF DESPAIR

A JOURNEY OF SELF-DISCOVERY
THROUGH JOURNALING & GOAL SETTING

Windi Floyd Reynolds

First printing, 2022.

Printed by IngramSpark, in the USA.

ISBN: 979-8-9871888-1-1
Independently published through Royal Ink Publishing
www.royalinkwriting.com

DEDICATION

With immense love forever and always, I dedicate this work to my Micah Bear, Macail, and Mike. Thank you for keeping me facing toward the light.

To the threads that complete me, my parents and siblings. Without you, my story wouldn't be this unique.

And to the magical beings that left this world sooner than our hearts expected, trajectories beyond our understanding. You were destined to be onlookers from afar, the shadows beyond the clouds, and our constant reminders to live life fully.

Eugena "Tisha" Holmes
4.27.1976 – 8.29.2022

Toraya Jai Garvin
5.6.2000 – 11.29.2016

I love you deeply, beyond this life.

When the sins of your father haunt you, where do you run and where do you hide?

Somewhere between light and darkness is where I tend to land.

Yearning for the light, yet somehow, always clouded by the darkness.

We all need a space
Free from judgment
Free from disapproving eyes
A space to be free
A space to think loudly
A space to be bold

We ALL need a space...

FOREWORD

This is for the old me.
The old me who wasn't present in her presence,
The me who couldn't focus in on the light of day
the moment,
the here and now.
So busy anticipating the next move,
The next reason,
The next.

This is for the old me who procrastinates,
who dibbles and dabbles,
Who isn't intentional about her intentions.
The me who spent so many years holding on to something forgiven so tightly
that she forgot how to love.
For the girl who couldn't be loved,
Shouldn't be...

This is for the possibility of the impossible in the girl, now woman, who is
determined to not allow her traumas to become generational.
This is for the woman who doesn't work for the pain of it all
& doesn't vacation in her anxieties.

This is for the woman who is living in a realm of reality where she shines in
the light and does not dwell in the darkness.
The woman whose 'sonshine' is so bright because he's given her some of the
most vital reasons to remain and to believe in the possibilities of her abilities.

And this is for YOU, the person who, though from time to time finds
themselves in between it all, is striving to be the change.

Our lives are created and shaped by a continual series of moments. How we move through the major moments of our lives can either enhance or restrict who we ultimately become. Finding ways to channel and control our emotions and thoughts in our present moments is essential if we want to avoid emotional explosions as we journey on to the next moment. It's the essence of inner peace. I know this, not because I'm an expert with fancy degrees from legendary institutions – though I do hold several. I know these truths because I have lived.

I have lived through not being the most popular girl in school. I've lived in hand-me-downs while my friends lived their lives adorned in the latest fashions. I've failed in school; I've excelled in school. I've gone from feeling like I didn't belong, almost like I didn't even exist at a predominantly white college to graduating from an HBCU, where I saw myself in nearly every facet of the experience. (Yes, I finally saw *me*.) I've felt like I was never going to find the perfect job. I've felt used, yet ignored and unheard, all in the same moment. I've managed teams both large and small. I've helped to raise another woman's child as my own. I've birthed a son. I've been on both ends of deception, feeling the bitter sting of each side. I have loved to the point of blind foolishness, and I have been loved unconditionally. Sometimes, I walk through my days afraid, unsure of where my next step will take me. I've fallen in love with sunrises while simultaneously dreading nightfall, not understanding that one doesn't happen without the other.

We all walk through life becoming more experienced than the day before. But how do we use those experiences without developing a "Me vs My Life" attitude? How do you use those moments (good, bad, and indifferent) to create a life you can be proud to live?

One way that I choose to channel my emotions and grapple with my life is through writing. I am a writer. Do the words come to me as eloquently as I'd like? Not usually. I'm no Maya Angelou or Toni Morrison; I'm me. And still I write. Mostly, the words come between the hours of near deep slumber and not yet awake. The act of documenting those words, whether on paper or electronic device, holds so much weight, and for me, in a moment of beautiful irony, a weight is removed. Whether it's the heaviness of years past or the burdens of the days to come, writing can help to alleviate some of the pressures that overwhelm the mind, body, and soul.

It's not surprising that writing, specifically storytelling, comes naturally to me. As a child, I fantasized – probably a little *too* much. I would create worlds all my own, where the characters were tailor-made just for me. And my young imagination was elaborate. Nothing short of romantic comedy montages (some real *When Harry Met Sally* type of stuff). I dreamt of meeting Harry or Hakeem all the time. It went something like this: We meet in a moment of fate disguised as happenstance, we fall in love, and it's all simple perfection – "happily ever after".

But there came a moment when I realized that real life isn't this big rom-com consisting of perfect meetups, the accidental sidewalk trip falling into a lover's arms, or love at first sight turned forever. As my experiences would prove, life was more like a soap opera, full of ups and downs, joy and pleasure, lies and deceit – a seemingly constant rotation of the same mistakes made, and wrongs corrected. (We'll get into those details.) In the meantime, let's walk through some key moments of my life as you journal moments from yours. I've found the power in writing things down. It can be truly therapeutic and has allowed me to reflect on who I was, who I am, and who I want to be.

FOCUS & REFLECT

Sometimes we must remind ourselves of who we are and just how powerful we can be.

- How would you introduce yourself?
- Using 'I' statements, describe yourself as you are right now. Re-introduce yourself to you.

MID THOUGHT

When I am stuck in a place I can't get out,
I write.
When I am held up by my own thoughts, fears and insecurities
I write.
Hoping to pen myself out of a dark place I've called home for way too long,
I will always write.

THE HERE & NOW

She's a girl
Often visits her past
Frequents her future
She's a woman
Hard pressed to understand
and to be present

ROSE COLORED DREAMS
NICKEL-PLATED REALITY

Lollipops, Sandcastles, and Fun
Childhood perhaps;
Pats on the back, kiddie games won
Childhood perhaps;
Not enough food, wish I had those name brand shoes
Childhood perhaps;
Unwanted touches, divorce views
Childhood perhaps;
If I wish hard enough upon a star,
I wonder if my entire childhood was a dream
Perhaps.

My earliest memory is from my preschool days, being served peaches on top of my cereal. I recall little kids, same size as me, running around, enjoying playtime. Everything seemed right. I didn't have a care in the world, and playtime was the highlight of my day. Enjoying my little kid life with my little kid friends was the best! Back then, friendships were formed through shared snacks and an excited "Hello!" on the first day of class. Life was just easy.

Those preschool to kindergarten years are vague in my memory. My recollection of early life becomes most vivid around first grade. My elementary school was like a fortress, equipped with a large staircase leading up to the front door of a massive brick building. It was old and had been standing strong, and long before I entered its halls. That building remains today and is now home to seniors in need of affordable housing. It's ironic really. An edifice that once nurtured our future's best and brightest now houses some of the greats of our past. This mighty fortress was where I once went to roam and learn. The building was probably only two or three levels high but, to a 1st grader, it was massive and filled with kids like me, anxiously awaiting each new moment.

Elementary school days are filled with so many firsts. Me and my tiny classmates, with whom I shared countless laughs and silly conversations, were unknowingly being nurtured and shaped into the grown-ups we would become. Strangely enough, I can't recall the names or faces of most of the kids who sat beside me each day as I learned to read and write. But I *do* remember the teachers. Ms. Gordon taught 1st grade. She was gentle in her approach and was a favorite of mine. Her skin was bright, her hair filled with curls. Not natural curls, but I assumed she added some sort of liquid activator, as so many of us did during that time. I smile when I think back on my own activated curls. Then there was Ms. Courts, my 2nd grade teacher. She had large breasts and wore a cone-shaped bra, like Madonna (but trust me, that's where the similarities ended). Ms. Courts was a stern lady. She ruled the halls. She was large in stature and stood tall, her voice loud and demanding. When she spoke to me and all the faceless children, we listened. Ms. Barnes was my 3rd grade teacher and a delightful transition from Ms. Courts. Her face was softer and much kinder. For as much as my memory holds, she was sweet and tender, Ms. Barnes.

I also remember the walks home from school. There were no car lines or school bus pickups. I walked to and from school alone. I clearly recall many long walks through my East Savannah neighborhood, several blocks between school and home, all the while trying desperately to avoid any stray dogs along the way; I had to make a run for it a time or two. Aside from the occasional run for my life, these were good times. My soul was filled with youthful glee.

The memories are few and fragmented, but the ones that stuck left a beautiful stain on my heart, a lasting imprint of wonderful childhood moments. Still, as I would learn, with most good times comes some bad. Sometime before 4th grade, life changed. After one of my lengthy walks, I arrived home to no electricity. My dad had it disconnected. I had homework to complete that day. We lit candles.

FOCUS & REFLECT

- Describe one of your fondest moments from your childhood.
- Can you recall how you felt at that moment?
- What are some of your most vivid memories about this time in your life?

Two Rooms

Two or three brick steps
A wooden door
Sprawling white carpet on the living room floor
Up ahead were two rooms
A long red crushed velvet like loveseat
To the left built-ins filled with photographs and encyclopedias from wall to
wall
As a kid looking up, it seemed over ten feet tall
But up ahead were two rooms
To the right, a dining room slash music room slash den
The room once filled with musical jazz teachings for the win
But up ahead were two rooms
Watch your step as you cross the hallway floor
A built-in floor heater, you might get burned
It happened to me, a lesson I seemed to never learn
But up ahead were two rooms
Long Kitchen counter
Landline on the wall
Call twice and hang up both times, not accepting calls
But up ahead were two rooms
Those two rooms housed us all
It's where we all slept
It's where we shared countless laughs, falls and secrets kept
A small space to share
A large space to own
5 kids, 1 bathroom
The morning time wait full of gloom
Up ahead were those two rooms
Behind me are some the best memories to ever bloom

The Seed

The absence of I love you can be damaging
Self-esteem grows from the roots of love
Stems of you are great and there isn't anything you can't achieve
sometimes broken and not seen
To be carefully watered by the feeling of love
provides the needed nourishment for a bud
Allowing growth which manifests in self love
translating into an intolerance of nonsense
Enabling the permission of a uniquely powerful and fearless YOU.

The Reason

I can't recall the deep conversations with my mother
Those thoughts blurred
Most vivid are the Sheppard pies and yummy smells from baked goods
White boy calendars on the wall
The introduction to No Doubt and Gwen
That little red jeep that carried us to and from many adventures
'Gotta Have Faith ah Faith ah Faith ahhhh' blazing from the jeep speakers
Me wanting to go everywhere you went
Until that one day when you got into that same little red jeep and drove
away for good

Sometime later I remember when flowers came in place of you
Honestly, there wasn't a bouquet big enough
And maybe that's the reason
I was hurt so much when you drove off that day
You were my foundation, you were my source and you poured into us all
I didn't just lose a sister
I lost my very first friend
My surrogate mother

Yet, what was lost when you left, was gained in a woman now free from the
bonds of her past
It took some growing and some learning to know that it was less about me
and more about you
Your time away seemed like forever and my hope has been that the time away
made up for all the years you allowed us to stand on you
We all stood on you as we peered out into the world for the first time
And maybe that's the reason
You had to go
You had to live
You had to simply be allowed to be you

And for all these reasons and so many more I pray those years of discovery
were everything you needed them to be because you were everything, I needed
during the discovery of me. That's the reason. Yeah, that's the reason.

1525

Long, red, covered driveway
Green, prickly carpet on the front porch
Plastic on furniture to preserve your best
Long, beaded strings…
I recall most of the noises upon entering the smallest kitchen ever
A deep, long den where the floor model TV sat
The largest master bedroom to date, dripping with a collection of your finest
An amazing structure
Crafted by my granddaddy to fit your perfection

1525
A million and one stories told
about how country life pushed you to the city
Some kids along for the ride and some kids left behind…
The story of many of times past, trying to find a better way
Domestic worker to flea market stands
Here. This. This is the place you called "Home."

1525

Single Mother

One Job
Two Jobs
Three Jobs
Four
The single mother plays a role of caretaker and so much more
A role carried alone
Some versions of help crept in along the way
My mother had one helpmate, two, three, let's say four
Lovers disguised as dutiful husbands but not much more
Seemingly by her side but still she stood mostly alone
The life of the single mother is a job where most of the hard work is done on
your own.
One Job
Two Jobs
Three Jobs
Four
The single mother
My single mother
I will forever be grateful forever more

As a kid, you always seem to want what another kid has. Even when you have everything you need, there's still the idea of something missing when you see that another kid has something you don't. Before my dad left, I lived in a two-bedroom house, shared among seven people. You can imagine there was probably a thing or two (or three) that I desired, but simply didn't have. To top things off, we lived next door to the Joneses – the actual Joneses – and they had everything, or so it seemed from the eyes of a kid who wanted "more".

The Joneses were the perfect nuclear family, complete with two kids, a boy and a girl. The dad had a solid job and spent time with his family. The mom was a stay-at-home mom. After my parents divorced, my mom regularly worked two jobs to support us. I didn't know many moms who stayed home as a way of life, so I gazed at the Jones Family in awe, as if stay-at-home mothers didn't exist literally all over the world. In my young mind, their family dynamic was a rarity, and I was amazed. Here was a real-life stay-at-home mom right next door to me. They were the envy of the block with their bi-weekly trimmed yard and long concrete driveway, big enough for several cars. I imagine their garage was filled with tools, toys, and bicycles. The only thing missing was a white picket fence. There was, however, a wire fence around their backyard, but we all had that. Aside from that small commonality, the Joneses had it all. The mom had this blue, big-bodied car that always stayed clean and was rarely ever driven. The dad kept it covered; I assumed to keep off the bird crap. I mean, why else?

I don't recall ever going into their house; there were never any sleepovers to speak of. I do remember, once or twice, getting a glimpse into their kitchen from the screened-in patio. It was the picture-perfect little kitchen, equipped with all green appliances. From the outside looking in, it looked to be the perfect place for their two kids to sit and enjoy daily made from scratch meals, which I was sure the Jones Mom prepared without fail. Their backyard was big and wide, and I did spend lots of time there playing with the Jones Girl. Her dad had built her a playhouse, and she would make mud pies all the time. She and I would play mostly with another neighborhood girl who lived across the street with her single mom, brother, and sister.

We were a dynamic trio...until, at some point, we weren't. You know how it goes. One day you're friends and the next moment, you aren't. Sometimes the friendships come back around; sometimes they don't. It's the story of so many young girls. But I'm drifting. The point is, the Jones Girl had a well put together family, while ours were what some would call "broken". And in a sense, compared to the Jones Family, they were. We were missing a dad in the home or missing the finances that would've afforded us some of the same things that the Joneses had. Their daughter's clothes were always the latest trends, while I wore more hand-me-downs than new arrivals. Both of her parents were present; meanwhile, my mom was always working at least 2 jobs, and my dad lived 7 hours away. I'll admit that feelings of jealousy and envy crept in a time or two. Keeping up with the Joneses was hard to do on a fixed budget. Nevertheless, there were always enough mud pies to feed the block.

FOCUS & REFLECT

- Who or what are you trying to keep up with, whether at work, school or play?
- Who or what challenges you to be your best?
- What are some of the steps you are currently taking to reach your goals?
- What do you need to implement that you have not already done, to reach a 3–5-year goal?

Real Estate

Oh, my. We found a summer home.
Industrial concept.
Equipped with four solid walls.
Running water.
Open floor plan.
Square footage for days.
Room for your vehicles?
Room for more?
Sold to the first bidder,
A family of four.

The Wash House

Rolls of quarters
Wash-n-Fold,
Those trips to the laundromat seemed to never get old.
Wire baskets
Rolling wheels
Trips to the laundromat were a biweekly sometimes weekly deal.
Great, big baskets filled with soiled clothes
So many metal tables to smooth out wrinkles, yet
nowhere clean to go and tinkle.
Big drums filled,
Going round and round
Washing clothes that had been stacked by the mound.
Headed back home
Clothes now so fresh and clean
Bags draped on the handle
Four pairs of peddling feet or a ride we would catch,
For we had done the job that needed to be done
The wash-n-fold.
A staple under the Miami night's sun.

I used to live in a warehouse. It was attached to a pager shop owned by my aunt and uncle. Along with housing the latest communication and tech devices, the warehouse also served as a dwelling for me, my sister, my brother, and my father. We literally lived in the warehouse. We ate, slept, watched TV, and made up dance routines to the hottest *Dance Party USA* songs. While it was business as usual in the front of the building, just behind the wall, there we were – living out our childhood. And we didn't have a care in the world. Although we never officially met, my neighbors were also business owners in a long line of other storefront shops, also with warehouses attached. I often wondered if any other families lived in those storage spaces.

I used to live in a warehouse. Our driveway was a long, concrete parking lot that was used primarily for truck drivers to deliver packages. Our front door was large and wide; it took two hands to pull it open and close. The inside was just open space. The floor was cold concrete, though I think we had a couple of throw rugs. The cooling system was a mix of fans, and because we were in Florida, we didn't need a heater. Our kitchen was a combination of the bathroom sink (for water), a small wash pan, and a hot plate on a table next to the TV. Now, how we took baths every day is up for debate. Any memories of long, hot showers or playing rub-a-dub in the tub elude me. It's very possible that we didn't take baths daily. But most kids hate bath time anyway, so we probably never considered it strange or even thought twice about it. My bedroom was a van parked inside of the warehouse, shared by my entire family. It was nicely equipped with a fold out bed, and I remember fighting over who would sleep in the middle section of the van. This middle part had two swivel chairs that we would face together to make a "twin bed" that could hold one person. The fold out bed was in the rear. The winner got the swivel seats, and the three of us who lost piled onto the fold out together to sleep.

I used to live in a warehouse. My backyard was the highway. (We were in the business district, so you can imagine.) McDonald's was basically right in my backyard…and what more could a kid ask for?! The grocery store was across the street. We literally lived in a modern-day walkable community, though it wasn't so modern at the time. We were sustainably living before it was even a thing. Living in the warehouse was normal for us. So normal, in fact, that I don't think I ever told my mother that a warehouse was one of the places we lived during the summers that we spent visiting my dad in Florida. After my parents divorced, she would send us to live with him during summer breaks. We lived quite contently in our humble warehouse – our summer home away from home.

FOCUS & REFLECT

- Growing up, what were some of the environmental challenges that you faced?
- Did you grow up with everything you needed, or did you feel you lacked the necessities?
- How did having or not having everything you needed affect you?
- Does it still affect you today?

Back in the Day

Super Nintendo, Sega Genesis
Big screen TVs equipped with mega satellites
Those were the days...
Holes in the ceiling
Cracks in the walls
Watch your step, you just might fall
Those were the days...
Ice cream trucks, endless food stamps supply
Cuban steak sandwiches, stuffed potatoes my, oh my.
Oh, those were the days...
Be in the house before the day becomes dim
Belts on my backside for reenacting sin
Oh, those were the days.

Two-Piece Meal,
All Thighs

I was so excited to hit the pool that day!

My two piece was new,

A towel wrapped around my frame to take me from my poolside seat to the edge of cool bliss.

The towel dropped…

Eyes locked in on me.

Fear emerged.

It rolled all over and through those walls of mine,

From the sole of my big feet to my thighs to the fringed tips of my nappy unkept hair.

What did those eyes see?

Why did those eyes choose me?

The immediacy of shame came over me and my towel followed.

I never wore a two piece again.

Rules Beget Questions

"Make sure you're back home by the time the streets light come on."
"Make sure you don't scream too loud."
"No, you can't play with the neighbor's kids."
"No, you can't hang with the crowd."
"Make sure you don't go past the corner."
"Make sure you don't leave my sight."
"Do you want me to give you something to cry for?"
"Hold out your hand, if you don't want a fight."

What were you so afraid of?
What a horrid life you must've lived
To protect and shield us from all the wrong you did.

During my summers growing up in Miami, we bounced around a lot. For a short time, my aunt let us sleep in one of her spare rooms on a bunk bed. We eventually made our home in an old, familiar place. On 53rd Street stood the house where my dad was raised. The neighborhood was called Brownsville or "Brownsub" …a family-oriented neighborhood. There were lots of young families there and a school nearby. My dad cherished this house. It was the place he called "Home" as a child. Despite the need for a major overhaul, it held a special place in his heart, and my dad made the house on 53rd Street home once again, as he had done with so many places before. That meant that it was now my home, too. The house was technically uninhabitable, and we weren't allowed to have friends come over – but not because we didn't want them to. Exactly the opposite. I, myself, yearned for the same interactions that other kids had, where it was a regular thing for their friends to come over and hang out – maybe even sleep over. Alas, there were no sleepovers on 53rd Street. Our home was not sleepover friendly.

As soon as you walked through the door, immediately above, you'd find a large piece of plastic attempting to hide the gaping hole in the roof. Below the hole, a chair and a lamp. There was a wide screen television to the right; to the left, a pull-out couch with one large cushion. Straight ahead was the dining room…not to be confused with a true dining room meant for actual family dining. Our dining room included a table completely covered with random items – newspapers, spare parts, boxes, etc. To the side, on a smaller table, there was a dishpan for washing dishes. Why a dishpan in the dining room? Well, it's simple really. That's where we washed our dishes. Further ahead, just before crossing the threshold into the kitchen, you'd find an old electric stove. The kitchen itself was a like a warzone and completely inoperable. We had to be careful where we stepped for fear of falling through the worn floorboards. Somehow, the refrigerator was salvaged, and it actually kept our food cold. And it never fell through the floorboards.

There were several rooms adjacent to the kitchen, but we stayed away. In these rooms, the floor and walls were both in horrible conditions. The walls had been worn down by the years, and the foundation needed major repair. To the right of the dining room (in a safer zone) was a bathroom and a bedroom. The bathroom was usable; there was a working toilet, sink, and tub. Though, when sitting in the bathtub, ridding yourself of the day's filth, you'd get a panoramic view of incomplete framing and exposed sheetrock. Next to the bathroom was our one usable bedroom. It was a safe haven of sorts. All four walls intact. No holes in the ceiling. The floor was solid. In this room, there was a bunkbed, a dresser, and a TV. And this is where we all slept – my dad, my brother, my sister, and me. This is where we played amongst ourselves. This is where we were disciplined and chastised, quite often for crimes we didn't commit. Spankings for screaming too loud, not wanting us to sound like "howling wolves". In this room, we cried. And we laughed. Though I couldn't see it at the time, this is where many of my life lessons were taught. Despite not having friends over, I recount many fond memories from that 53rd Street house. Sega levels conquered. New television shows discovered (courtesy of one of the largest satellites I'd seen, found in our very own backyard). Funny enough, my dad wasn't focused on home improvement, but he was rather big on always having the latest gadgets and electronics.

As I reflect now, I suspect that house had been holding on to years of happy memories long before I ever lived there. No wonder my dad wouldn't walk away, and instead chose to live in the 53rd Street house in the face of such conditions. It was still home. He did eventually walk away many years later – by force.

My mom never set foot inside our Miami home away from home, so she had no idea of its conditions. And we never mentioned a thing to her about how we were living. Every fall, we would return to our home in Savannah as if all was well and it was perfectly normal to live in a house where the floors were caving in. I guess when you're a kid, you don't realize something is broken until someone tells you that it is.

FOCUS & REFLECT

- Growing up, did you ever keep a secret from your parents that you may not have revealed to them until after you were an adult?
- What impact did keeping that secret have on you growing up?
- Does it still affect you now?

The Race

I ran so hard to not be a young girl

I mean I sprinted

No dilly No dally

I ran so hard to not be a young girl

I was ready

I was ready for what the world had in store

I ran so hard to not be a young girl

And then life came and flew by me so fast

Sixteen, Eighteen, Twenty-one, Twenty five, Twenty six….. plus more

I ran so hard to not be a young girl

The sprint turned marathon

The dilly dally turned reality check

I ran so hard to not be a young girl

Until the race was won

As a child of divorced parents, I spent a lot of time traveling back and forth between them. The seven-to-eight-hour drive between Savannah and Miami was long. We would hit the road at the end of each summer, always with our "5 school outfits a piece" quota from Marshalls in tow. More often than not, we would travel via US 1 versus Highway 95. I hated US 1 when I was a kid. Simply put, it was the long way home. Nevertheless, my dad would always say that he took that route because there were more gas stations just in case his van ran hot. Essentially, the service stations and stores along US 1 provided an endless line of resources as we journeyed along.

Now that I'm older, I like to think of my time spent on US 1 a metaphor for life's journey. I've learned that having a support system can be critical as you move towards a fulfilling future. The line of resources and the access that you have to those resources is integral. Resources will come in all shapes and forms – from your immediate family, your network of friends, or even a random stranger. And your resources extend beyond people. They can obviously have monetary value, and that value can increase or decrease depending on how you steward and invest your money. Resources can come from the educational opportunities you take advantage of. All in all, the resources that you have access to can greatly affect how you move through the journey of life.

As a kid, I would have preferred Hwy 95, as it was the quickest route to my destination. However, I've learned that immediate gratification, or taking the *shorter* way, isn't always the *best* way to success. There are times when we must take the long way, often for our greatest outcome. At times, we'll have to really nurture our relationships. Networking and cultivating mutually beneficial relationships can be a slow process. Still, however slow, when it's mutual, it's usually worth it. The acquisition of life's resources –

human, monetary, or otherwise – is necessary to build a solid personal foundation. Fulfillment is as much the journey as it is the destination. As you travel along, despite the speed of that journey, attach yourself to what builds on your foundation and ultimately, to what fulfills you...creating a space where you feel supported to be you.

First and foremost, you are your number one resource. Self-support comes from the inside out. Your journey may take you down some dark and lonely roads. Long and strenuous roads. It may feel like you'll never get to where you want to be. That's the time to stop, take a moment, and turn to those resources that you've picked up along the way. Reach out to those people who make you feel supported and have the ability to pour into you. Remember the personal enrichment things that you've acquired, from traditional education to unique skills and life experiences (ones that you may have taken for granted) and use them to make something magical happen for yourself.

And yes, there will still be times when you feel as though nothing is changing. But as you take inventory of your available resources, don't forget to look inward. Personally, when I get to a point where I feel like no one can help, or even understand, I pray. I feel peace in prayer. I feel seen and heard in prayer. I feel supported. I feel guided. I take the time to walk myself through life and pray for directions along the way. No matter how long it takes to get to your destination, be sure to fill up on positive energies and beneficial knowledge. Release the negative vibes, frustrations, and guilt from times past to make room for new moments. Don't sit and stew over how long it's taking. Travel the distance for the sake of traveling. Travel the distance for the purpose of catapulting yourself to a higher level with each step you take. Give yourself grace. Life is the longest, shortest journey you'll take. Learn from it. Grow from it. But above all, enjoy it!

FOCUS & REFLECT

- What resources have you discovered along your journey?
- Who supports and lifts you up in life?
- What tools or resources have you utilized to get you to where you need to be?

You've Been on My Mind

You've died in my thoughts so many times

I've grieved and mourned you

Shaken

Anxious

Alone

In these thoughts of which are just my own

Some live for the day and enjoy their moments

Some live for the day and embrace what is

I seem to wait for the day

The Call

The Final Answer

The Oh Yeah I Knew This Would Happen

But why couldn't

Why didn't you get away?

It never happens exactly that way

Muted

Your attempts to mute me don't go unnoticed
To live a life less lived because you are not able is not just
You douse my spirits
You ask me to live less fulfilled
If life is not to gaze onto and immerse oneself in HIS greatest creations, then
what is life?
Your attempts to mute me don't go unnoticed
But notice them, oh no more

Life Flight

Inward thoughts turn to outward shame when residence is allowed
Self-doubt does nothing for the under cherished soul
Less often than enough self-reflecting on the great things accomplished
Constant overthinking on what has not
Childlike tendencies when attempting to find the right footing
Life gets complicated
One step at a time, right?
A faux truth in the belief that we live arms wide open
Ready and willing to embrace what's next, the endless possibilities of life
Still gripping on much too tightly to the past
In search of a prefabricated existence
To be validated by the unknown
Forward moving in theory but stuck
Life gets complicated
One step at a time, right?
From the inside looking in
I am enough
The better part of me is not lost
Oh how the negative winds of the world try to beat me down
My foundation is rooted in No's, Abuse, Neglect, and Disregard
The time has come
I must use the core of my struggles to see, to live, to thrive, to grow
A moment of liberation
The steps I've taken were to get me right where I am now
Despite current circumstances
Mind wide open
Present complexities of the world are at my feet
I am here to seize my thoughts
One step at a time

In Defiance of the Darkness

Faith, many say is a belief in the unknown
Minds, hearts and extroverts ready to spontaneously combust
Not knowing when this crisis will truly end
Because who's to say when it's really over

The isolation
The insanity of it all

Faith, it appears to mean testing the lines of the invincible you versus the
mortal me
A hoax, a conspiracy, a masquerade in disguise
Disregard of social rules and distancing cues
Because they can't tell me it's over

The ignorance
The inconsistencies of it all

Faith, some say works in mysterious ways
Bodies, souls and spirits now at rest
Having to pass on without a hand to hold
Because they said it was over and this time it was

The inhumane
The incomprehensible nature of it all

Faith, it means we meet again
Paradise, heaven, nirvana or simply an unconsciousness state
We survive with the hope
Because when it's over, it's not really over

The immeasurable

The infinity of thought, after all

Have faith in the unknown, knowing all well that's how we make it through
to the light and defy the darkness

The Expectation of My Perception

You beat me down with doubt
You don't believe in me
You look at me with shame
You speak negatively

Born into this world, perhaps with not enough self-confidence instilled
Single handedly grown from a mother
Her too, raised by another, where she too was not celebrated
You see inadequacies deeply ingrained
Yet, there's a part of me that knows I am more than what you think
But I cannot find the will to believe it so

You are me
I am you
The voice inside
It guides us through
Yet, there's a part of me that knows I am more than what you think

I beat myself down
I look at myself with shame
I speak negatively about myself
The level of self-sabotage is insane
Yet through portals of time
Discoveries of the soul
Hard hit with life truths and becoming more aware of its duplicitous dealings
Rooted in self hate
Covered in brown bag scrutinizing
Topped with "You would be a better version of you if" idolizing

You see now I am woke
I see more in me now than ever
I am my representation
I stand for me
I was born beautiful, not perfect or without sin
I was created amazingly yet not without faults

I have raised the expectation of my perception, I celebrate me
Not merely adequate, Exceptional.

I am more because I said and believe it's true.
And now you, me and I know it too.

South of Wonderland
North of Despair

Where am I?
Where will I be?
I'm always stuck somewhere in between

My thoughts never allowed to just be happy
Always thinking of the worst to come
Restricted by some unrestricting unknown
Bound by the what if and oh yeah that always happens

Where am I?
Where will I be?
I'm always stuck somewhere in between

I thought and I thought
I thought so hard and began to wonder
Is the place I belong, is that place right here in me?
Bound by no bounds if I just let myself free?

Where am I?
Where will I be?
I'm always stuck somewhere in between

A supernatural force placed at birth
Placed within to be outwardly shown
But clouded by thoughts of very my own
Bound to keep me in despair

Where am I?
Where will I be?
I'm always stuck somewhere in between

This place of wonderland is a magical spot
I will fill it with thoughts of wonder
Shatter what once didn't allow me to be free
Because guess what my dear
The Magic is ME

The Conundrum of the Anxious Mind

Often, the anxious mind causes us to wonder about the whys,
Not allowing separation from then and now.
Thoughts of defeat...
Extreme distance found between our true destiny and the falsities of the world.
Thoughts of winning, doubtful...
Fear frequently taking over.
Thoughts of conquering the day, unknown...
A glimmer of hope sprinkled throughout each second, each minute.
Constant decisions to be made when you are simply just trying to seize the day.

TODAY, WHAT SPACE ARE YOU IN?

DATE: _____

OUT HERE WANDERING, WONDERING . . .

◇ WHY ARE THINGS SO STAGNANT?

◇ WHY ARE THINGS MOVING SO SLOWLY?

◇ WHY IS MY LIFE SO STALE?

◇ WILL THINGS EVER CHANGE FOR ME?

◇ _____

◇ _____

◇ _____

I WONDER BECAUSE

_____

_____

_____

_____

_____

_____

_____

_____

_____

_____

TODAY, WHAT SPACE ARE YOU IN?

DATE: _____

◇ DOUBTING

◇ DOUBLE DOUBTING

◇ TRIPLE DOUBTING

◇ DOOM STAYS AT MY DOOR

Doom stays at my door...
They say opportunity comes knocking.
Hopefully, it stops by once more!

I FEEL THIS WAY BECAUSE

FROM DESPAIR TO WONDERLAND
(VERBAL CONFESSIONS)

I AM AFRAID.

I AM ANXIOUS.

YET, I AM READY FOR CHANGE.

I HAVE DONE THE THINGS NEEDED.

I HAVE PLANNED.

I HAVE PREPARED.

I KNOW THAT

I AM THE BEST VERSION OF ME.

I JUST HAVE TO

OUTWARDLY SHOW IT THROUGH THE

ACTIONS AND DECISIONS THAT I MAKE

PERSONALLY AND PROFESSIONALLY.

I WILL BE SEEN.

IT'S IN HOW I WILL CONFIDENTLY CARRY

MYSELF.

IT'S IN HOW I WILL CHOOSE TO USE MY

VOICE.

I AM STILL AFRAID...

YET I KNOW THAT I AM EVERYTHING AMAZING.

DEAR ANXIOUS MIND,

I AM HERE TO RECLAIM
THIS DAY.
WITH ZERO REGRETS!

SIGNED: _____

MY FEARLESS SOUL

FREE THOUGHT

We all need a space
Free from judgment
Free from disapproving eyes
A space to be free
A space to think loudly
A space to be bold

We all need a space
Not bound by the rules
Not bound by tradition
A space to be unique
A space to be a rule breaker
A space to redefine the lines

We all need a space
That's says - YES you are amazing just as you are
That's says- YES you are the definition of what you should be
A space to be all the wonder
A space to be magical
A space to be YOU!

Use the remaining spaces in this book to express your thoughts of both DISMAY and WONDER.
It's your free space to plan, goal set and simply EXPLORE!

THOUGHTS OF DISMAY

THOUGHTS OF DISMAY

THOUGHTS OF DISMAY

THOUGHTS OF DISMAY

THOUGHTS OF DISMAY

THOUGHTS OF DISMAY

THOUGHTS OF WONDER

THOUGHTS OF WONDER

THOUGHTS OF WONDER

THOUGHTS OF WONDER

THOUGHTS OF WONDER

THOUGHTS OF WONDER

GOALS
&
MAGICAL PLANS

GOALS & MAGICAL PLANS

GOALS & MAGICAL PLANS

GOALS & MAGICAL PLANS

GOALS & MAGICAL PLANS

GOALS & MAGICAL PLANS

GOALS & MAGICAL PLANS

"FREE SPACING"

JUST EXISTING.
NULL OF THOUGHT
AND
NUMB TO IT ALL,
NEEDING TO BE REPLENISHED...

SOUTH OF WONDERLAND

A JOURNEY OF
SELF-DISCOVERY
THROUGH JOURNALING
& GOAL SETTING

NORTH OF DESPAIR

ABOUT THE AUTHOR

Windi Floyd Reynolds in an author and the owner of Focused Ink Group, LLC. A two-time graduate of Savannah State University and a Savannah, GA native, her journey as an author began in 2017, but her love for writing has always been present. Her debut publication "To Raya With Love", earned Reynolds an Indie Author Legacy Award nomination, and she continually seeks to inspire others to reach for their dreams.

Reynolds currently works as a certified healthcare professional in Jacksonville, FL. Through Focused Ink and the therapeutic art of journaling, she hopes to reach the world.

"Focused goals lead to a focused journey."

~ Windi

https:// www.focusedink.com   ✉ focusedink@gmail.com   📷 @focusedink